A Question of Technology

Can You Break the Internet?

and other questions about THE INTERNET

Clive Gifford

Gareth Stevens PUBLISHING

**Please visit our website,
www.garethstevens.com.
For a free color catalog of all
our high-quality books, call
toll free 1-800-542-2595 or
fax 1-877-542-2596.**

Cataloging-in-Publication Data
Names: Gifford, Clive.
Title: Can you break the internet? / Clive Gifford.
Description: Buffalo, NY : Gareth Stevens Publishing, 2027. |
Series: A question of technology | Includes glossary and index.
Identifiers: ISBN 9781482478464 (pbk.) | ISBN 9781482478471 (library bound) |
ISBN 9781482478488 (ebook)
Subjects: LCSH: Internet--Juvenile literature.
Classification: LCC TK5105.875.I57 G544 2027 | DDC 004.678–dc23

Published in 2027 by
Gareth Stevens Publishing
2544 Clinton St.
Buffalo, NY 14224

First published in Great Britain in 2023 by Wayland

Credits:
Editors: Julia Bird; Julia Adams
Design and illustrations: Matt Lilly
Cover design: Matt Lilly

Picture credits:
Getty Images: Karjean Levine/Archive Photos 18; Andreas Rentz 3c; Helen H Richardson/MediaNews Group/The Denver Post 27c; Miguel Ropa/AFP 28t. NASA Johnson: 2b. Shutterstock: Boyisteady 17t; Javier Brosch 14-15; Business stock 24b; Iinspiration 19t; Damir Khabirov 22b; Oleksandr Lytvynenko 11t; Melica 24t; Lal Nallath 20b; Redpixel.pl 19b; SerPhoto 8t; Diego Thomazini 13; Zentilla front cover, 1. Wikimedia Commons: Bajan64-commonswiki CCA-SA 4.0 International 3tr; Scientist-100 PD 3tl.

Printed in China
CPSIA compliance information: Batch #QS27GS: For further information contact Gareth Stevens at 1-800-542-2595.

Contents

WORLD WIDE WEB

WEATHER -3 °C
BUT YOUR
COAT IS BEING
DRY CLEANED,
SO WRAP UP
WARM!

What is the internet?

The internet is a kind of network. A network is created when two or more computers are linked so they can share information, known as data.

The internet is the ultimate in linking things together. It is a network of networks. Using shared rules, known as protocols, millions of digital devices can communicate with each other, sharing information all over the world … and beyond.

Astronauts in space enjoy out-of-this world internet access.

Who runs the internet?

The amazing answer is no one! Although users may have to behave according to national laws, there is no one person or organization in overall command.

Cyber champs

No one person can take credit for inventing the internet. It was developed over time by many smart, dedicated people, including these three legends.

Radia Perlman
(1951–) invented ways for computers to share data faster and more reliably, which are still used on the internet today. Epic!

Tim Berners-Lee
(1955–) invented the entire World Wide Web. What a legend! (Turn to page 18 to find out more about him.)

Alan Emtage
(1964–) invented the first internet search engine in 1990. This made it much easier to find files and data.

What has the internet done for us?

A lot! The internet has revolutionized the ways people work, play, learn, and gain information.

Web surfing
Video calls
Online shopping
Online schooling
Multi-player gaming
App downloads
Online banking
Email
Smart TV
Virtual courses and digital libraries
Live streaming
Social media
exchanging photos and videos
Cashless payments

Are the World Wide Web and the internet the same thing?

NOPE!

They're quite different.

The **INTERNET** is a network of computer networks.

The **WORLD WIDE WEB**, or Web for short, is one application (use) of the internet. Email is another example of an internet application.

Making connections

The internet's connections are the physical cables, switches, and routers between computers, as well as the transmitters and receivers that connect devices using radio signals.

The Web's connections are between different webpages. They're not made by cables and switches, but by computer code called hyperlinks. These direct users to different webpages, images, and sounds on the Web. Each has its own address, called a URL.

At your service

Webpages are stored on a server computer. When you want to view a page, you send a request over the internet to the server, which sends the page back.

So, no internet = no request or response!

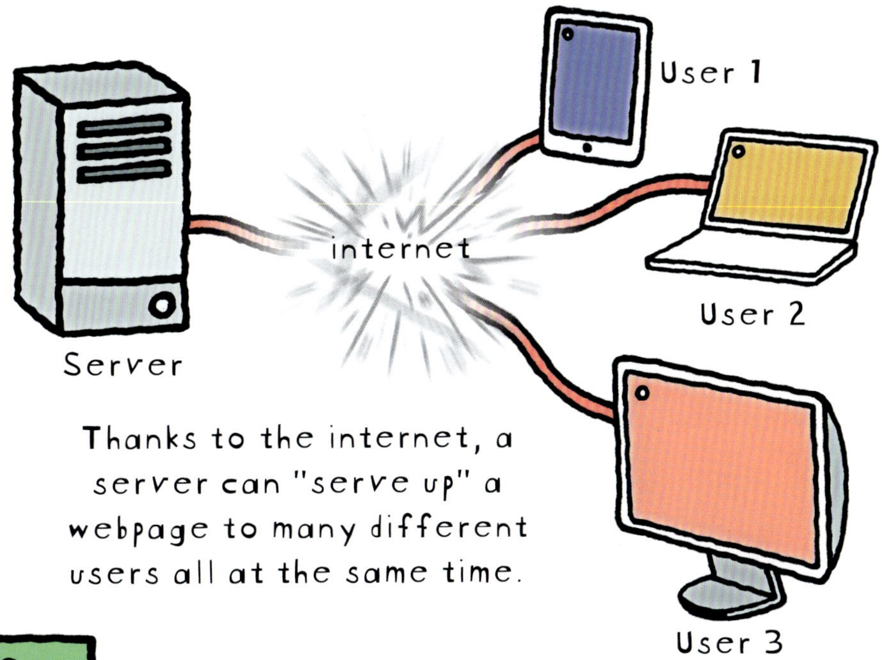

Thanks to the internet, a server can "serve up" a webpage to many different users all at the same time.

Two-way street

The Web may rely on the internet to work, but it has also made the internet far more popular and exciting. With the Web's arrival in 1990-91, people could easily share and enjoy information and multimedia. The number of websites and internet users boomed!

How many websites are there?

It depends on when you read this, as an estimated 100-200 new websites are created every minute!

What we DO know is that after a slow start, website numbers truly exploded.

1991	1992	1995	2000	2010	2022
1	10	23,500	17,087,182	206,956,723	ca.1.8 billion

What was the first thing sent over the internet?

Have a guess. Was it a cute cat photo? A funny joke? A great music track?

Nope. It was just two letters, "l" and "o."

It was meant to be "login," but the network couldn't cope and crashed. Oh dear.

Fortunately, things improved.

Building up

The first network was called **ARPANET.** In 1969, it linked just four computers in different locations in the United States. It's grown **A LOT** since!

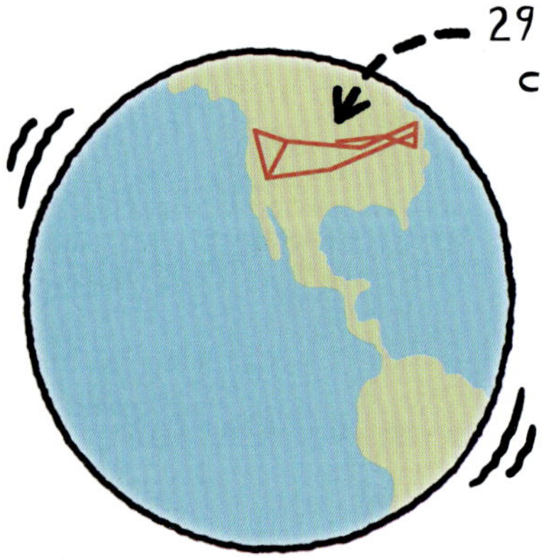

1972: 29 computers connected

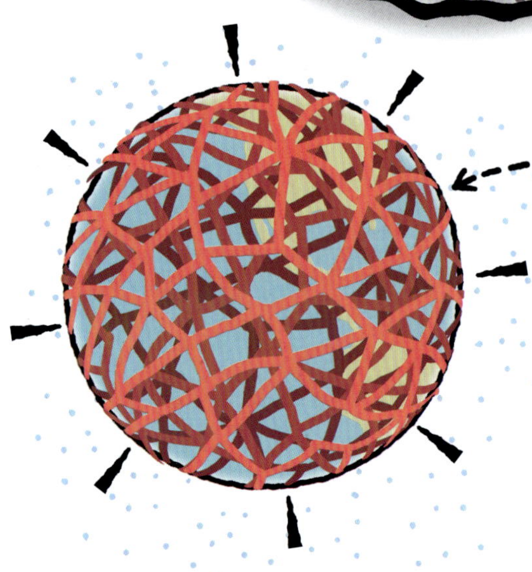

2022: 22 billion+ devices connected

1992: First photo uploaded on the Web

Text success

At first the internet was mostly used to share text or computer code-based items. The 1990s and 2000s saw **HUGE** changes as pictures, sound, and videos could now be sent over the internet, and websites and social media developed.

1993: First webcam

1994: First downloadable song

1995: Amazon and eBay arrive as websites

1998: Google search engine launches

2004: Facebook launches

2005: YouTube starts sharing videos

2006: Twitter launches

2010: First photo on Instagram

So what did people do before the internet?

The internet is such a big part of our lives today, it might be hard to imagine life without it. Here are a few examples of what people did before the internet existed.

Instead of instant messages, people sent postcards and letters.

Friends visited to show photos or play music.

Physical copies of movies or music were bought or rented.

The closest thing to social media was the school or club noticeboard!

Information came from books, newspapers, and magazines, as well as news programs and documentaries on TV.

Voice calls were made on landline telephones.

Can the wind blow WiFi away?

Sounds possible, doesn't it? After all, wireless signals from your laptop or tablet travel through the air. So does smoke, and it can be blown off-course by a gust of wind.

Rapid radio

But no, it's not possible. WiFi consists of invisible radio waves that cannot be blown away by winds. They also move far faster than a storm can ever dream of – up to 186,272 miles (299,775 km) per second! That's **RAPID!**

WiFi's enemies

Not that WiFi's perfect. Its waves can be weakened when traveling through thick concrete walls. Radio wave signals can also be messed up or blocked by other devices that give off similar electromagnetic waves, such as TVs and WiFi's number one enemy …

MICROWAVE OVENS!

Why wireless?

WiFi was developed in the 1990s and launched in 1997 as a way of connecting to the internet without using wires.

It allowed portable devices like tablets to use the internet while on the move. Lots of public places – from libraries to parks – created WiFi hotspots, offering easy internet access. Today, more than 20 billion devices use WiFi to connect to the internet.

So, how does WiFi work?

A wireless router, linked to the internet, sends and receives data as radio signals over short distances.

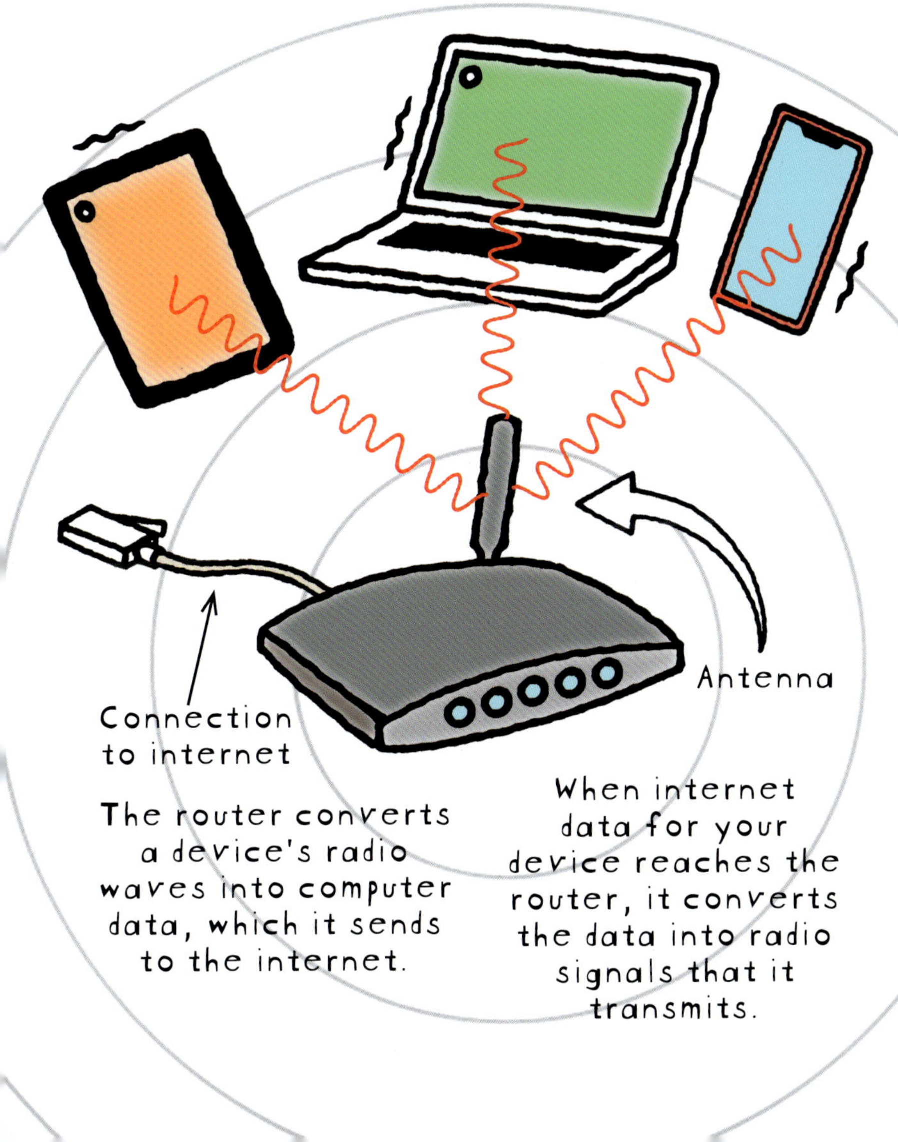

What does WiFi stand for?

Nothing in particular. Honest. In fact, it had other names before WiFi.

Is the Web really full of spiders?

Yes, it is. Spiders (not real ones though!) are vital to how a search engine works. Without search engines, trying to find what you need on the gigantic World Wide Web would be pretty much impossible.

Creepy-crawlies

Spiders, or web crawlers, are programs that constantly travel the Web. They visit every webpage and analyze its keywords (which describe the page and its contents), then add the page's URL to their index.

A spider's work is never done. They all patrol the Web forever and revisit webpages that may have changed. As they do this, they build up a truly ENORMOUS index of billions of pages.

Spiders then follow the page's hyperlinks and visit every webpage it's connected to. This helps build up a clearer picture of what the website is about.

Match-making

A search engine takes your question or keywords and whizzes through its **GIANT** index at frightening speed. It uses sets of rules called algorithms to help it make matches.

These may consider your location, especially for a request such as "cafés near me," or will look up what your past searches were to help narrow down what it thinks you're after. It doesn't always get this right, which is why you should:

Always examine a lot of the results, not just the first few.

Repeat your search with different, clearer descriptions.

Results!

Once it's made its matches, the engine ranks its results and displays them to you in order. Sometimes, companies pay for their results to be shown at the top. Each result is hyperlinked, so one click and you're away.

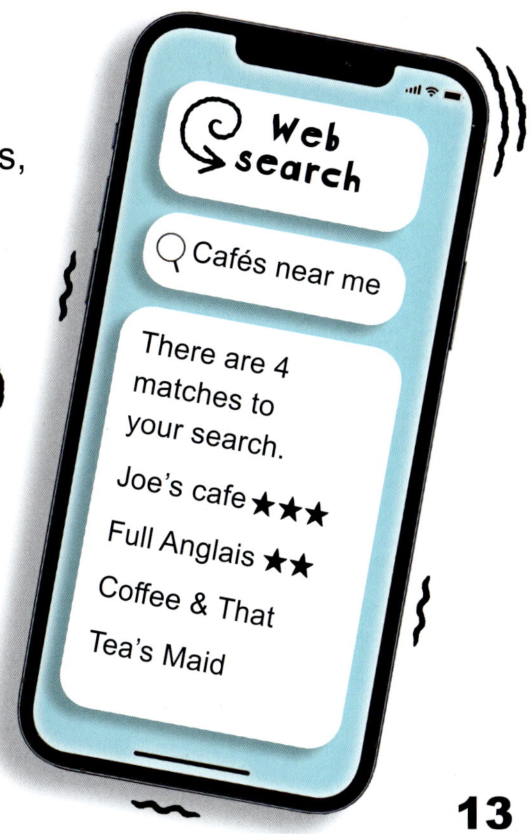

Major search engines are marvels. In 2022, the Google search engine was handling 8.5 billion searches a day. And it's all thanks to spiders!

Is there one big internet superhighway?

No, there's no one route all internet data travels on. Nor is there a giant tunnel under the ocean that all emails and video streams head through to travel between continents.

Shame, as that sounds fun.

Instead, that funny photo of a surfing dog you sent to friends ends up going on quite a journey …

Split up

Actually, make that journeyS. Why? Because your data is split up by computer software into small, manageable chunks, called packets.

Each packet is labeled with the address of the sender and where it's going. Then it is whisked off across the internet.

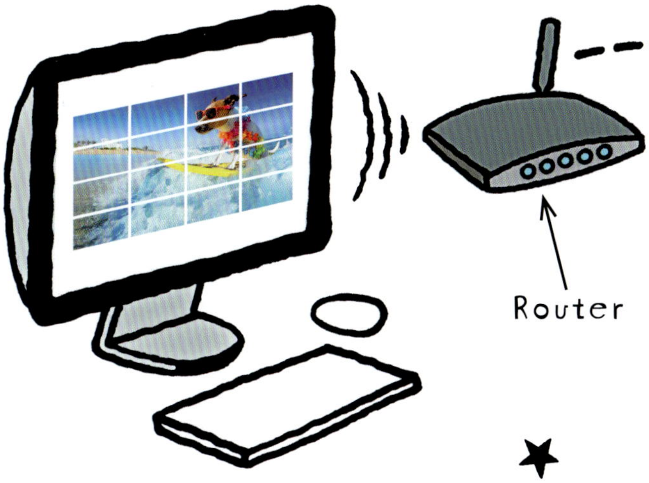

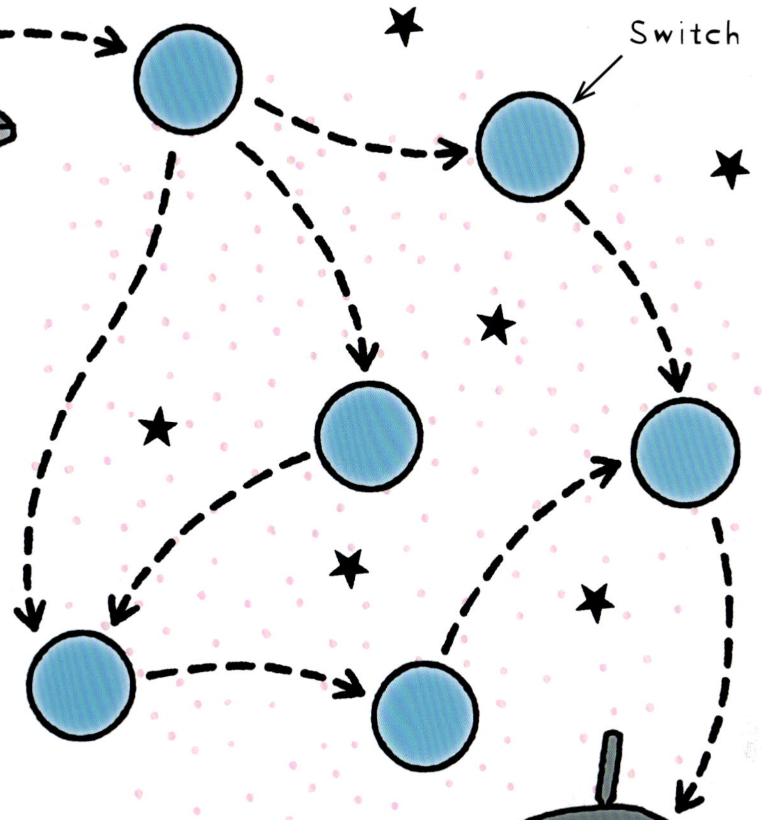

Byeeee!

The packets don't follow each other head-to-toe like a truck convoy. Instead, they each go on separate and, often, completely different journeys.

Devices called **ROUTERS** and **SWITCHES** direct the packets across the internet based on what the best and quickest route is at that moment. When the packets reach their target, they are all put back together to form the original data.

If a packet is missing, it can be resent more quickly and easily than resending the entire file.

All this can happen in thousandths of a second. Pretty amazing, huh? The whole process is called **packet switching** and it helps computer networks run reliably and well.

Why does the internet need walls?

A lot of people believe the internet shouldn't have any barriers, but others feel they're necessary. Firewalls protect users against online attacks, for example, while paywalls protect content.

Hack attack

The internet has given criminals and bullies new opportunities to attack, steal, and vandalize. They may do this by sending viruses or other harmful code over the internet that steals your personal data or disables your computer. **SCARY STUFF**.

Firewalls are sometimes machines, but mostly computer programs. They check arriving internet data *before* it is allowed through to the rest of your computer. Only internet traffic from trusted sources gets in.

Many firewalls filter every single packet of data that arrives, checking each against a long list of threats and untrusted sources.

Stay safe

Apart from firewalls, you can stay safer on the internet by only using trusted websites and never downloading unknown files or giving out your personal details, especially passwords.

A password is like a toothbrush: choose a good one, don't share it, and change it regularly!

Free forever?

It takes a lot of time, effort, and expense to build a good website and keep it stocked with fresh, new content. Some companies, especially newspapers, now charge people a fee to access their websites.

The barrier they erect is called a paywall and it can only be overcome after paying for access.

Over the limit

Some paywalls are soft. This means that the website keeps track of how many visits you make, articles you read, or files you download. You're allowed a small number for free before the paywall comes crashing down. **THUMP!**

But don't forget, most websites still remain free and there's **A LOT** of great, safe stuff out there.

Why is TimBL an HTML Hero?

Tim Berners-Lee, known online as TimBL, is a British computer engineer. Computing runs through his family – his parents met while working on one of Britain's first successful computers, the Ferranti Mark 1.

It featured hyperlinks – symbols or words on screen which, when clicked on, took you to different pieces of information.

Smart directory

In the 1980s and 1990s, Tim worked at the Swiss science center **CERN** where he invented an ingenious computer-based address book to keep track of the 10,000 or so staff.

In the late 1980s, Tim tried to apply his address book worldwide so that people could place their documents on the internet and any computer could access the information. This led him to make **FOUR CRUCIAL INVENTIONS**.

1 HTML

Tim created HyperText Markup Language (HTML). This computer language is used to turn pages of text (and later, pictures) into exciting webpages. With some improvements, HTML is still used today.

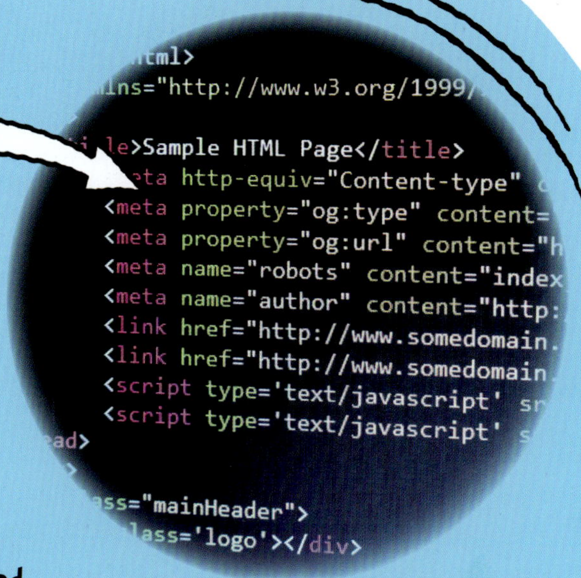

2 Web server

He stored the webpages on a dedicated computer called a web server.

3 HTTP

Tim developed a set of rules and techniques so different computers and devices could ask for and receive webpages. Called HyperText Transfer Protocol (HTTP), this helped make webpages available to all.

4 Web browser

To ask for webpages and move between them using the hyperlinks, Tim wrote the first Web browser, a computer program that lets you view and navigate websites.

With those four strokes,
Tim pretty much invented the World Wide Web. **AMAZING!**

The first website went live to the public in 1991. Today, anyone with a computer, tablet or smartphone, Web browser and internet access can visit billions of webpages by simply clicking hyperlinks.

Do I need rainboots to go streaming?

No, you'll be fine in your slippers or bare feet! Streaming is the sending of a constant flow of data rather than a complete file. It's used to provide music, audiobooks, TV, and movies to people using tablets, computers or smart TVs.

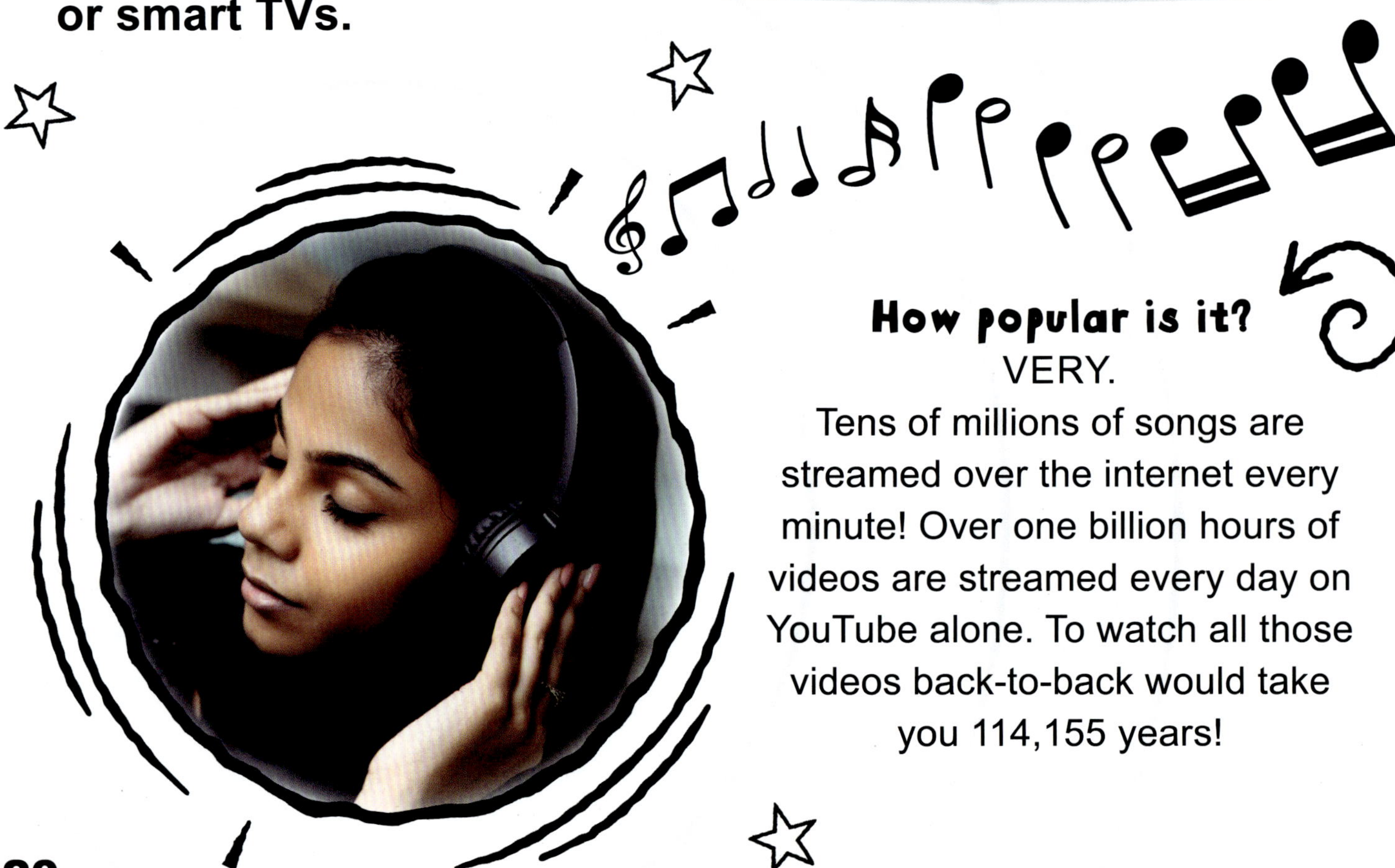

How popular is it?
VERY.
Tens of millions of songs are streamed over the internet every minute! Over one billion hours of videos are streamed every day on YouTube alone. To watch all those videos back-to-back would take you 114,155 years!

Can't you just download the whole thing?

Yes, but high-resolution video and sound files can take a long time to download and occupy a lot of memory space. With streaming, the data disappears after you've finished watching or listening.

This is how it works:

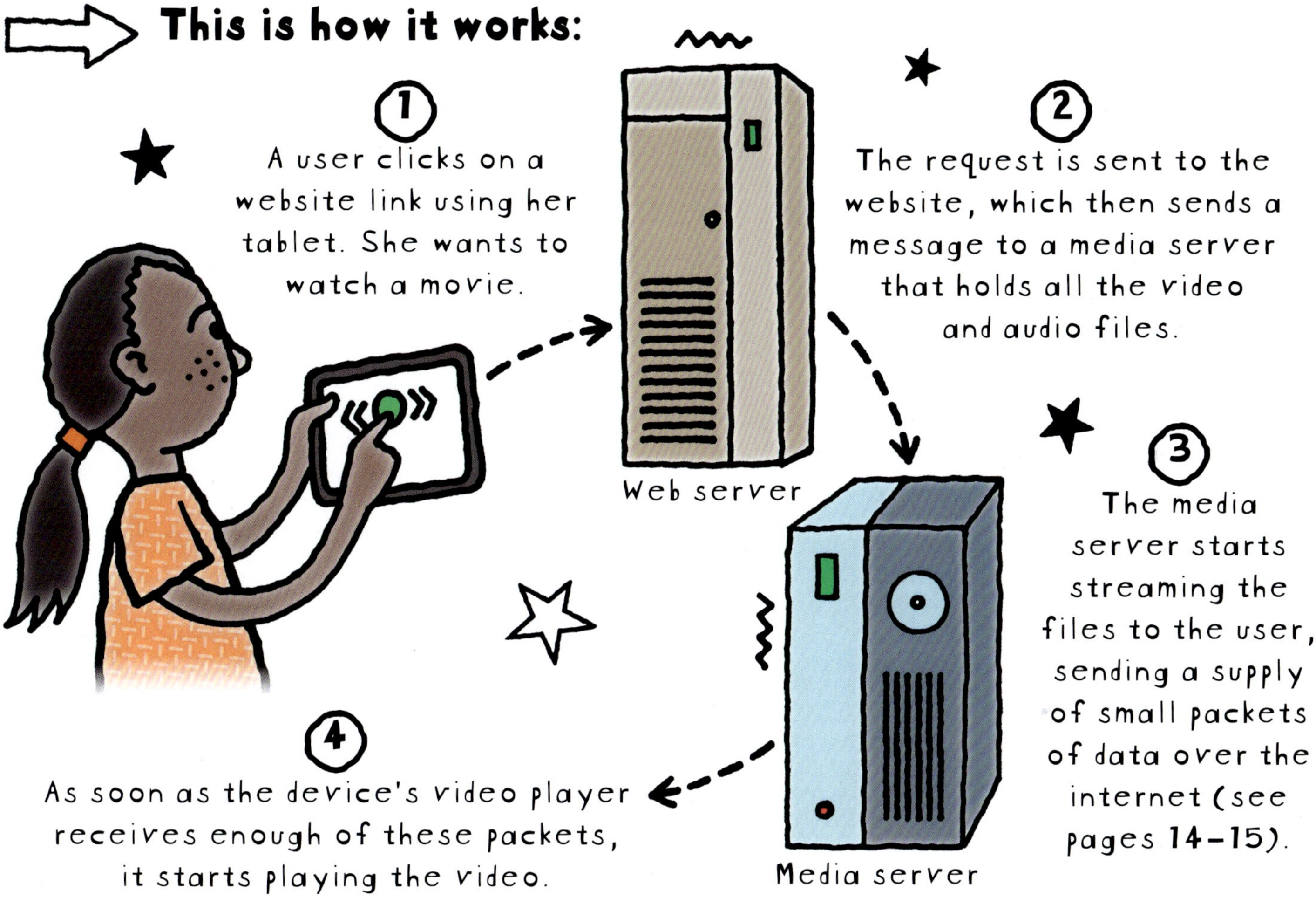

Hitting the buffers

A slow device or internet connection can sometimes see a stream stop for a few seconds to wait for the packets to catch up. This is called **BUFFERING** and it can be annoying.

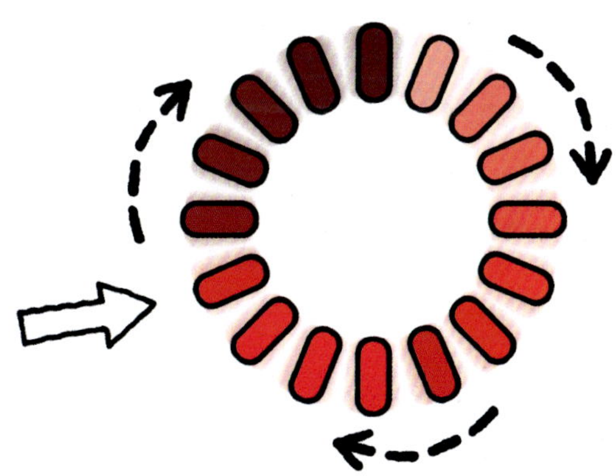

<< Rewind

After it has played, a packet of data is deleted from the user's device. Does this stop the user rewinding and replaying parts of the stream? No, the computers simply instruct the media server to re-send those packets in an instant.

Can you break the internet?

You hear that phrase a lot, but all it really means is that a story has "gone viral" and is the talk of the Web that day. But the extra traffic isn't actually going to damage the internet. In fact, not much is, short of a worldwide power cut!

Lots of links

Remember, the internet is a big **COLLECTION** of computer networks. Some networks or important links between major networks, known as exchanges, are run by government organizations, others by companies.

But all have their own safety features, including back-up power supplies and servers to keep outages to a bare minimum.

And if one network, exchange, or link between networks breaks down, there are usually plenty more to take their place.

Routing for you

Packet switching (see pages 14–15) also helps to make the internet more robust. When there's a problem with one network or a part of the planned route, switches and routers simply redirect the data along a different path to its destination.

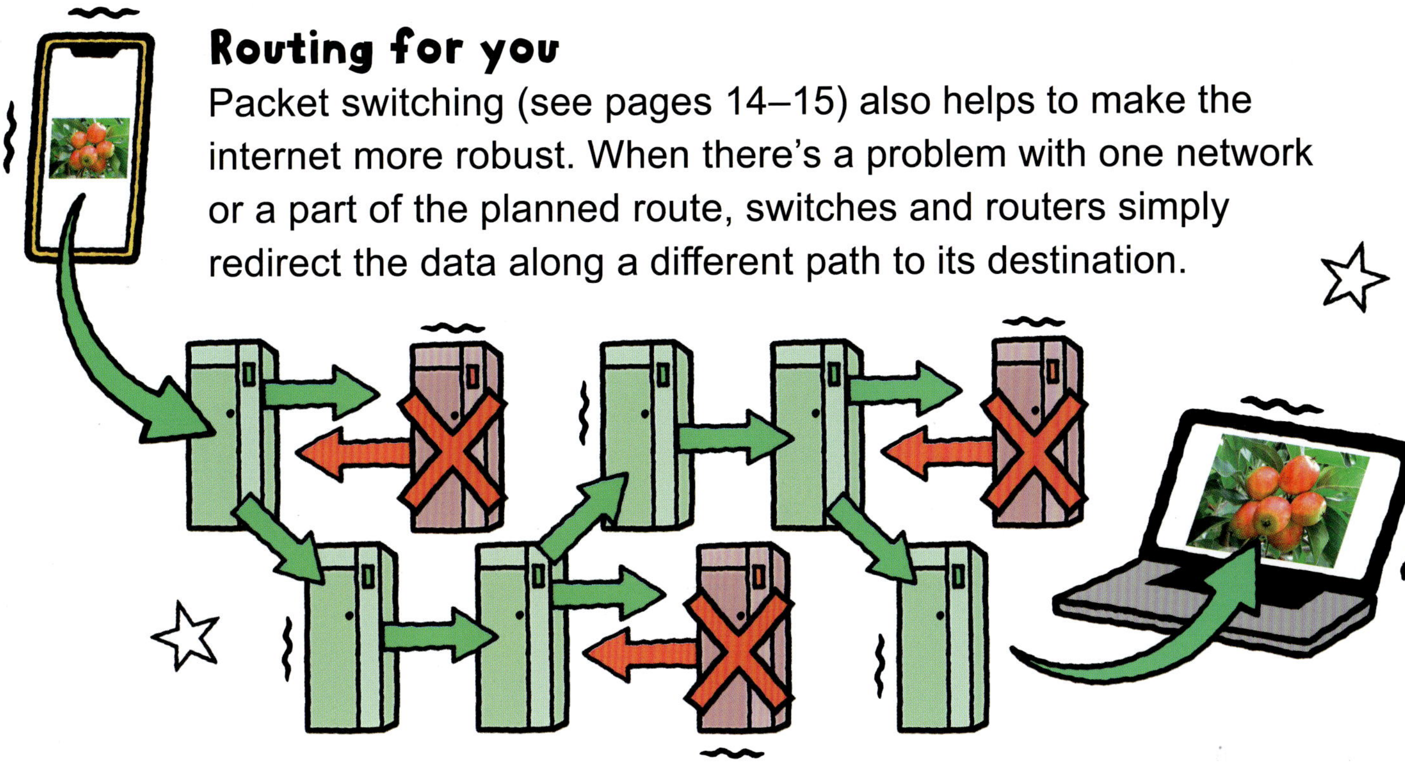

Net threats

Not that there aren't problems and threats that keep some internet experts awake at night.

These include DoS – denial of service – attacks where a website or network is targeted by hackers. The hacker's programs send millions of requests to a server, overwhelming it and blocking out requests from regular users.

Below the surface

Much of the world's internet traffic between continents is carried by slender fiber optic cables. A damaged cable is a worry. However, as there are more than 745,000 miles (1.2 million km) of internet cables on the ocean floor, there are usually alternative routes available.

What's the Internet of Things?

It's no longer just devices that can link to the internet. The Internet of Things (IoT) refers to all the other objects, from fitness trackers to toasters, that connect to the internet.

Did you say toaster?

You bet! In fact, a toaster became one of the very first IoT devices when computer scientist John Romkey placed a modified appliance online in 1990. Users could control browning levels and, by 1991, even lower the bread into the toaster using a mini crane.

What's inside?

IoT devices contain microprocessors, circuits, and wireless transmitter-receivers, allowing them to share data over the internet with other IoT devices or their owner. They can be controlled remotely and send alerts via smartphone apps to owners long distances away.

Connected homes

IoT devices are making homes smart, more energy-efficient and safer:

Door can alert the owner if it's not locked and send videos of visitors to a smartphone.

Mirror displays personalized news, alerts, and weather forecasts.

Heating and lighting can be controlled using an app.

Smart plugs turn off unneeded power to save energy.

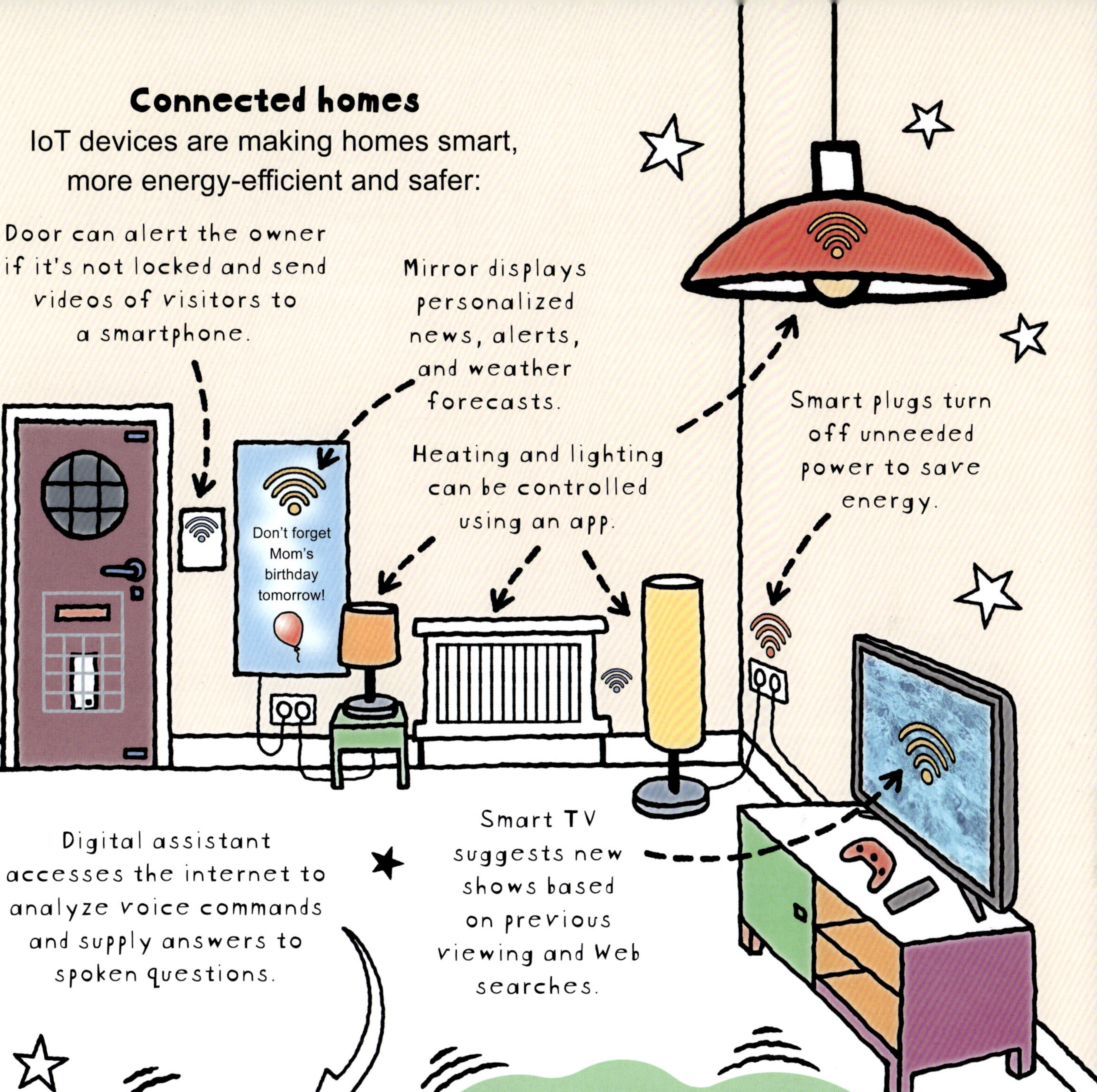

Digital assistant accesses the internet to analyze voice commands and supply answers to spoken questions.

Smart TV suggests new shows based on previous viewing and Web searches.

It's not just at home

Connected cars hop on the internet to obtain up-to-the-minute details on traffic, construction, and parking spaces. They can also automatically pay road tolls and even diagnose upcoming problems and repairs.

What's the digital divide?

In 1990, only 1 in 200 people (0.5 percent) used the internet.

Today, that figure has soared, but there remain many who have no access to the internet. The gap between those who have access and those who don't is called the digital divide.

How many

A whopping 4.95 billion people currently use the internet. Sounds impressive, but that's less than 64% of the global population. So, over a third of all people don't have access.

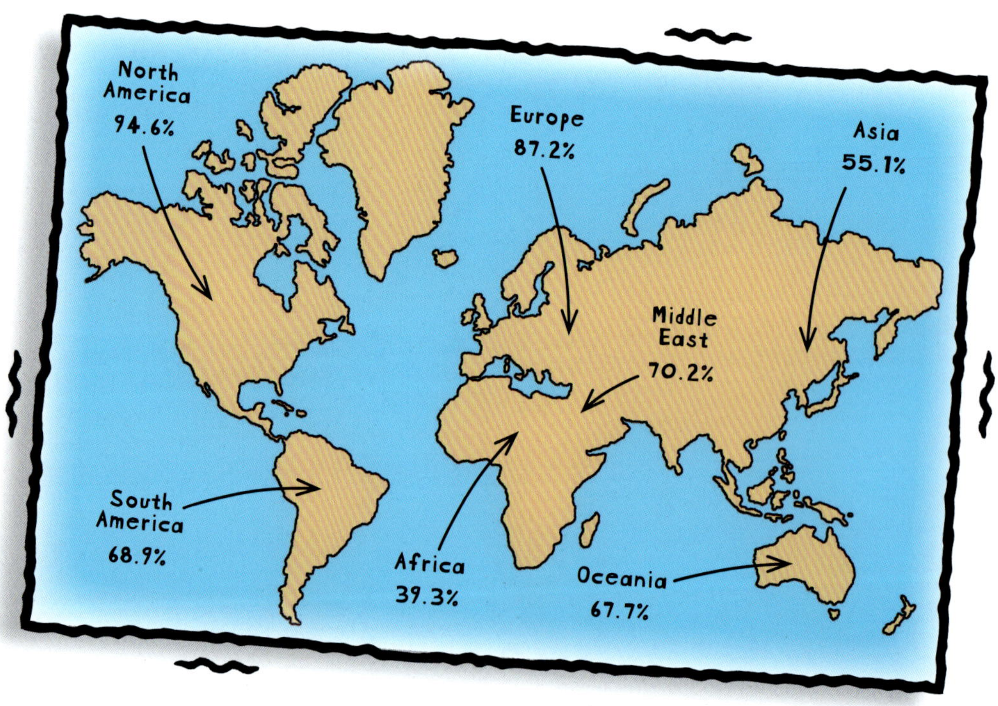

As the map shows, the biggest divides are found in Africa and Asia, home to many of the world's poorest communities. The African nation of Eritrea has the lowest of all – just 7% of its population have internet access.

Is it just a problem in poor countries?

Nope. Internet access is also limited in some wealthier countries, especially in rural areas and among the elderly and poor. In the United States, around 8 million people do not have internet access at all in their homes.

Bridging the gap

The internet welcomed 240 million new users in 2025. That's good news, but there's so much more to do.

Some groups are donating tech to poorer regions or bringing internet access to hard-to-reach places using wireless radio masts or satellite dishes.

It's electrifying!

Many isolated places still lack electricity. So, plans to electrify rural communities are important. Wind turbines, solar panels, and generators that run on plant-based fuels can provide electricity in these remote areas.

Quick-fire questions

Why's there an @ in my email address?

You can thank an American computer programmer named Ray Tomlinson. He sent the first email over the internet in 1971. He wanted to separate the email sender's name from the host – the computer they were using to send the message – and choose the @ (at) symbol.

What's the difference between an IP and an ISP?

An ISP or Internet Service Provider is a company that connects your devices to the internet, usually for a fee. An IP or Internet Protocol is quite different. It's a unique code that identifies every individual device connected to the internet.

Why was it called the World Wide Web?

Because it seemed like a good idea at the time! Tim Berners-Lee and his colleague Robert Cailliau racked their brains. They considered The Information Mine, The Mesh, and Mine Of Information. Eventually Tim decided on World Wide Web because a diagram of connected computers looked like a web.

What do server farms grow?

Data! And lots of it. These facilities consist of thousands of server computers, each storing huge amounts of data. Server farms are needed to store all the billions of webpages, email accounts, records from online stores, and messages sent by social media. Server farms use a lot of electricity and some farms are **big, big, big!**

Glossary

App Short for "application." A small computer program such as a game that can be downloaded and used on tablets, smartphones, and other mobile devices.

ARPANET An early computer network, formed in the United States, considered to be the internet's starting point.

Browser A program that lets you call up and display websites and search through them.

Download When you copy information that is located on another computer to your own computer, such as when you download a game from the internet.

Fiber optic A type of cable that carries signals rapidly along fine strands of glass.

Firewall A protective barrier, usually one or more computer programs, that protects a computer from unwanted access.

Hackers People who use computers to get unauthorized access to your computer or digital device and its data.

HTML Short for Hypertext Markup Language, this is a computer coding language made up of tags that people use to mark up a document to turn it into a webpage.

Internet A giant computer network of smaller computer networks that allows people to send, receive, and share data with one another.

Memory Part of a computer or other digital device in which information can be stored.

Microprocessor A complete computing unit on a single chip that can perform thousands or millions of operations per second.

Network Two or more computers or digital devices linked together in some way so that they can communicate with one another.

Packet A small block of data that is transmitted across a computer network.

Router A device that connects two or more separate computer networks and forwards data to other routers in different networks.

Server A computer that stores data, which can be accessed on request.

Social media Online communities where you can connect with friends, family, and other people who share your interests.

Upload Send a computer file from one computer to another, or, if connected to a network, post the file on the network for others to share, view, and use.

URL (Uniform Resource Locator) A unique address for each file or webpage held on a computer network such as the internet.

Virus Malicious program or piece of computer code that spreads from one computer to another by email or through websites.

WiFi Wireless network technology that allows people to connect computers and other digital devices to each other and the internet.

Further reading

Websites

developer.mozilla.org/en-US/docs/Learn/Common_questions/How_does_the_internet_work

A useful guide to parts of the internet.

computer.howstuffworks.com/web-page.htm

A relatively detailed look at how webpages and websites work.

www.youtube.com/watch?v=x3c1ih2NJEg

A nine-minute-long video showing how data travels around the internet from servers to devices.

www.sciencemuseum.org.uk/objects-and-stories/arpanet-internet

Learn more about the history of ARPANET and early computer networks.

www.youtube.com/watch?v=LVV_93mBfSU

A great video on how search engines work, brought to you by Code.org.

Books

Inspirational Lives: Tim Berners-Lee: Creator of the Web

by Claudia Martin (Wayland, 2017)

Get Ahead in Computing: Webpage Design

by Clive Gifford (Wayland, 2019)

From an Idea to Google

by Lowey Bundy Sichol (Clarion Books, 2019)

The Big Book of Invisible Technology

by Chloe Taylor (Rockridge Press, 2020)

Create the Code: The Internet

by Max Wainewright (Wayland, 2021)

Index